UNCONSCIONABLE CONTRACT

WHAT CREDIT CARD COMPANIES DON'T WANT YOU TO KNOW

by

Jana Lynn Shellman

DEDICATION

I dedicate this publication to all of the instructors I've studied under, and to all of the attorneys who have employed me, and thank them for their patience and understanding, as well as their forbearance in allowing me to continuously think outside the box.

©2011 Threadbare Publishing Co
a subsidiary of
The Wish Factory, Inc.
318 W. Leith Street
Fort Wayne, IN 46807-1439

INDEX

UNCONSCIONABLE CONTRACT
What Credit Card Companies
Don't Want You to Know

I found myself in circumstances beyond my control, out of a job with credit card debt close to $40,000.00 in 1997. My only asset was time on my hands and a history of nearly forty years as a paralegal with a strange (to most) love of reading case law on my coffee breaks.

This is my story of what I learned about Credit Card Companies, how I stopped them from harassing me when I found I couldn't pay them off, and how I counter-sued them when they filed suit against me, and how, ultimately they all agreed to "call it even".

DON'T TRY THIS AT HOME!!

I don't recommend this solution for the average creditor who has not had extensive legal experience. If you want to try it, find yourself a lawyer with the time and the zeal to pursue this, and if you find your circumstances are similar to mine. You should discuss it with an attorney. It isn't easy. Again, if you believe some of the solutions might work for you, you should seek the advice of an attorney in that regard. Furthermore, nothing contained in this book should be construed as legal advice, or steps that could be taken by you.

Unconscionable Contract   by Jana Lynn Shellman

MY STORY

You might be wondering how I amassed nearly $40,000 worth of credit card debt in the first place. I was working as a paralegal and earning a fair amount of money at the time. I had just gotten a divorce, and I was supporting a teenage son with the help of child support from his father. I left the marriage with the house, the mortgage, and credit card debt from the marriage. It was a fairly equitable division of property and debt, inasmuch as I also received a payout of our liquid assets. The credit card debt I assumed from the marriage amounted to about $5,000. I paid that off almost immediately, and the credit card company was so ecstatic they doubled my credit limit and other credit card companies started throwing cards at me. I soon had five or six cards.

Then I had a couple of windfalls. Actually they were injuries. First I was hit in the mouth with a frisbee on the beach at Lake Michigan. It knocked loose a couple of teeth. The people I was with grabbed the kid who threw the frisbee, and the consequences of that injury were that his guardians' insurance company offered me close to $20,000.00 for the injuries I'd sustained. I paid off the credit card debt I had accumulated to then, and paid cash for an off-lease vehicle. (I still have that car, by the way, and it's old enough to vote, but a very reliable vehicle with lots of miles yet to go on it.) The credit card companies were thrilled and they all doubled my credit limit once again.

A year or so later, I was working very hard, hurrying here and there to accomplish all of the duties of a paralegal helping to run a law office, raising a teenager and keeping a house. The day before Christmas I hurried into a grocery store and tripped over a rug that had been caught and bunched up in the automatic door, causing me to suffer a permanent injury to my back that has resulted in a pinched sciatic nerve and neuropathy in my feet. I have little or no feeling from my ankles down to the bottoms of my feet. My boss helped me to negotiate a settlement with the grocery store's insurance company and I received another lump sum settlement. I paid off the credit card companies and they, once again, doubled my credit limits.

The following year I started taking a course in the evenings to acquire a real estate license. I passed with flying colors, and while working as a paralegal in the law office, I also joined a real estate firm to sell houses on weekends and evenings. I wasn't a very good salesman but I found a love of finding good deals, and buying houses.

Along with a couple of partners, I invested in a couple of houses which we acquired from the city for a small amount of money. We invested cash into renovating those houses and I eventually sold my interest and recouped my investment. I used the cash to pay off the credit card companies once again and, you guessed it, they doubled my credit limit again!

In 1995 I had formed my own publishing company and had published my first book, The Wish Factory: How to Make Wishes Come True. I had continued to work as a paralegal and a real estate agent, and I worked very hard on publishing the book, attending book fairs around the country, purchasing merchandising advertisements, and all of the costs of publishing. A lot of my credit card debt was for the printing, publication and promotion of the book.

I continued to work and pay off my credit card debt as I went along, and I had excellent credit. Then in 1997 due to circumstances over which I had no control I didn't have a job anymore. I was fifty-six years old, and no one wanted to hire someone my age. I'd never had a problem like that before.

The eternal optimist, when I ran out of savings, I continued to use my credit cards to buy essentials, pay for my son's education, and attempt to promote my books and sell houses.

On October 2, 1997, I cut up my credit cards, and sent letters to each of my creditors.

That should stop the harassment, but it doesn't always work. By the way, if you choose to send this letter, keep track of any calls that occur within a day of your having received the return receipt card showing they received your letter.   You are going to need it later. It is part of your evidence of their harassment. Having this record bolsters your defense. Keep a log, with the date, time, and the name of the card company, and if you can get it the name of the caller. I used the line, "may I please have your name, so I can add you as

8

a party to my lawsuit?" That in itself sometimes ended the harassing calls. Until they sold it to another collection agency.

The letter follows:

Date

Credit Card Company
Address
City, State, Zip:

RE;   NAME OF CREDIT CARD, ACCOUNT NUMBER #

Gentlemen:

Please be advised that due to circumstances beyond my control, I am no longer able to make any payments on my credit card debt to your company.

Please stop all telephone calls to me, my employer (if any), my friends, my relatives, and/or my neighbors. You may contact me by mail if you have anything to tell me.

I remain optimistic that I will once again be able to meet my obligations, but I cannot predict with any reasonable certainty when that event might occur. In the meantime, please honor my written request and desist from any further telephone calls from you and your agents or assigns.

Thank you.

                                    Signature

It wouldn't hurt to send this letter by certified mail, return receipt requested. Keep a copy of the letter, and attach your mailing proof to it immediately, and when the card is returned attach it as well. Keep it in a file with your bills. You may need it.

<u>Unconscionable Contract</u>   by Jana Lynn Shellman

WHAT CAN YOU DO?

You can stop the unwanted telephone calls immediately by writing the letter to the credit card company. The only thing wrong with this is that they then send it to a collection agent who ignores the letter. Keep track of this. They are supposed to notify the collection agency that you've written the letter.

Unconscionable Contract   by Jana Lynn Shellman

<u>MY STORY CONTINUES</u>

I spent most of 1997 writing, trying to sell houses, going through my savings paying off debt with all I had left and living off of what I got in unemployment benefits.

When I ran out of money it didn't take long for the credit card companies to begin harassing me.

I began reading case law to find out how I could stop them from their continuous harassment. In the process I learned a lot.

I read the Indiana Statutes with regard to collections, and with regard to contracts, revolving charge accounts and consumer credit.

Every state has Statutes which govern their commercial law, as well there is the Uniform Commercial Code with regard to the laws of commerce, which includes credit purchasing.

Following are a few of the things I read:

Unconscionable Contract   by Jana Lynn Shellman

FAIR DEBT COLLECTION PRACTICES ACT

Fair Debt Collection Practices Act prohibits debt collectors and collection attorneys from using undue harassment and other unethical practices when collecting debt.

What debts are covered?

Personal, family, and household debts are covered under the Act. This includes money owed for the purchase of an automobile, for medical care, or for credit cards.

How may a debt collector contact you?

A collector may contact you in person, by mail, telephone, or fax. However, a debt collector may not contact you at unreasonable times or places, such as before 8 a.m. or after 9 p.m., unless you agree. A debt collector also may not contact you at work if the collector knows that your employer disapproves.

15

Can you stop a debt collector from contacting you?

You can stop a collector from contacting you by writing a letter to the collection agency telling them to stop. Once the agency receives your letter, they may not contact you again except to say there will be no further contact. The agency may notify you if the debt collector or the creditor intends to take some specific action.

May a debt collector contact anyone else about your debt?

If you have an attorney, the debt collector may not contact anyone other than your attorney. If you do not have an attorney, a collector may contact other people, but only to find out where you live and work. Collectors usually are prohibited from contacting such permissible third parties more than once. In most cases, the collector may not tell anyone other than you and your attorney that you owe money.

What must the debt collector tell you about the debt?

Within five days after you are first contacted, the collector must send you a written notice telling you the amount of money you owe; the name of the creditor to whom you owe the money; and what action to take if you believe you do not owe the money.

May a debt collector continue to contact you if you believe you do not owe money?

A collector may not contact you if, within 30 days after you are first contacted, you send the collection agency a letter stating you do not owe money. However, a collector can renew collection activities if you are sent proof of the debt, such as a copy of a bill for the amount owed. (Request that they send written proof, including your purchases, and your signature on any charges purportedly made to any account.)

What types of debt collection practices are prohibited under the Fair Debt Collection Practices Act?

--Use of threats of violence or harm against the person, property, or reputation

--Publishing a list of consumers who refuse to pay their debts or advertise your debt (except to a credit bureau) or give false information about you to anyone

--Repeatedly using the telephone to annoy someone or telephone people without identifying themselves

--Falsely implying that they are attorneys or government representatives or misrepresent the involvement of an attorney in collecting a debt

--Falsely implying that you have committed a crime and will be arrested if you do not pay your debt

--Giving a false name when they contact you or falsely represent that they operate or work for a credit bureau

--Misrepresenting the amount of your debt or claim they will seize, garnish, attach, or sell your property or wages, unless the collection agency or creditor intends to do so, and it is legal to do so

--Indicating that papers being sent to you are legal forms when they are not or indicate that papers being sent to you are not legal forms when they are or send you anything that looks like an official document from a court or government agency when it is not

--Claiming that actions, such as a lawsuit, will be taken

against you, which legally may not be taken, or which they do not intend to take.

--Collecting any amount greater than your debt, unless allowed by law

--Using obscene or profane language

--Depositing a post-dated check prematurely

--Taking or threatening to take your property unless this can be done legally

--Making you accept collect calls or contacting you by postcard

--Calling your employer, neighbors, friends and relatives and revealing your delinquency to them [A delinquency can be revealed to a co-signor.]

Note that the Fair Debt Collection Practices Act regulates debt collection agencies and attorneys and does NOT apply to original creditors.

However, most major creditors have adopted collection

policies that do not violate the Fair Debt Collection Practices Act.

Original creditors are regulated by state laws which might closely follow the Fair Debt Collection Practices Act. Therefore, if a debt collector's conduct violates the FDCPA, there is a good chance it also violates laws in your state.

If you believe a creditor is harassing you or violating the law, look up your state's laws regulating creditors' collection activities on the Internet. You can complain to your state's Attorney General's office if you feel a creditor has violated state law.

****

I read the Fair Debt Collection Practices Act. I read everything I could put my hands on. Then I read the equivalent information for my state. In doing so, I found that there was a state law that said creditors on installment contracts could only charge a $5.00 late fee at that time. I took advantage of that knowledge and incorporated it into my writing.

20

STRUGGLING WITH MORAL ISSUES

I was initially reluctant to renege on what I considered to be my obligations to the people I "owed". However, in the process of discovery in the law suits, I found I had already fulfilled my obligations to them. I had purchased goods and services, for which I had fully compensated them, and then I had paid them interest in an amount that any reasonable person would consider a good return on their money. I no longer felt guilty. Even after all that, they collectively claimed I owed them a lot more money. I decided to argue. My polemic proclivities persisted. Surprisingly not one of the credit card companies ever answered any of my letters, of which I had kept copies, and proof of mailing in the form of return receipt cards signed by someone at the credit card companies.

Anyway, at some point that year, a couple of the credit card companies decided to sue me. I sued them back. That is, when I got their Complaints, I immediately answered their Complaints, made my Affirmative Defense, using every Affirmative Defense I could find in the situation,   and then I   made Counterclaims against them suing them back for unconscionable contract and harassment.

THINGS I LEARNED IN THE PROCESS

After I filed my Answer with Affirmative Defenses, and my Counterclaims, I received Interrogatories from the Attorneys for the Creditors.

They were standard Interrogatories, asking me to divulge all of my information. I turned around and sent them Interrogatories, demanding that they send me copies of any and all contracts that I had signed. In the process I learned a couple of things:

First, credit card companies don't keep copies of the "application" you made for the credit card. They do not have your signature on any contract of any kind whatsoever. Neither do they keep copies of the slips you sign when you make purchases. In other words, there is no contract with the credit card company. They don't have your signature on anything. They only keep copies of your bills for about two years, if that long.

Unconscionable Contract   by Jana Lynn Shellman

.

WHAT ARE THE ELEMENTS OF A CONTRACT?

Legal Elements of a Contract

The essential elements necessary to form a binding contract are usually described as:

• An Offer
• Acceptance
• Consideration
•Terms that cannot be changed without the consent of both parties in writing.

Offer

An offer is defined as the manifestation of the "willingness to enter into a bargain so made as to justify another person in understanding that his assent to the bargain is invited and will conclude it.

Acceptance

Acceptance of an offer can occur in several ways: Acceptance of an offer is a manifestation of assent to the terms thereof made by the offeree in a manner

25

invited or required by the offer. An acceptance must not change the terms of an offer. If it does, the offer is rejected. A material change in a proposed contract constitutes a counteroffer, which must be accepted by the other party.

The offer must be clear and definite just as there must be a clear and definite acceptance of all terms contained in the offer.

To be enforceable, the parties must have agreed on the essential terms of the contract.

Full agreement on all contractual terms is the best practice and should be the norm. It is only when an essential term is left open for future negotiation that there is nothing more than an unenforceable agreement to agree. Such an agreement is void as a contract.

Any contract or mutual understanding between parties that differs materially from the original offer is open to legal challenge. Should any component of a negotiation tend toward a final result where a contract or agreement differs materially from the offer, that component of the negotiation should cease. If the component in question is critical to

the provision of a service or goods, the issuance of another offer that incorporates that component should be considered.

Certainty of Subject Matter

In general, a contract is legally binding only if its terms are sufficiently defined to enable a court to understand the parties' obligations.

The rules regarding indefiniteness of material terms of a contract are based on the concept that a party cannot accept an offer so as to form a contract unless the terms of that contract are reasonably certain.

Thus, the material terms of a contract must be agreed upon before a court can enforce the contract. Each contract should be considered separately to determine its material terms.

Consideration

Consideration is an essential element of any valid contract. Consideration consists of either a benefit to

the promisor or a detriment to the promisee. It is a present exchange bargained for in return for a promise. It may consist of some right, interest, profit, or benefit that accrues to one party, or alternatively, of some forbearance, loss or
responsibility that is undertaken or incurred by the other party.

It is not necessary for a contract to be supported by a monetary consideration.

Competent Parties

Parties to a contract must be competent and authorized to enter into a contract.

HOW DOES THIS APPLY TO CREDIT CARD TRANSACTIONS?

Offer: You receive the credit card application in the mail. Okay that's an offer.

Acceptance: You, or anyone else for that matter can simply stick a return address label on the application and send it back. In most cases, they don't even ask for a signature on the card. You are simply accepting the offer of the credit card itself. You are not signing anything, and they haven't signed anything. (Or somebody else accepted it for you. No signature, no proof. We once had a client who never applied for credit cards, but someone applied for credit cards for them sent to another address.)

You have not negotiated a contract unless all of the terms of the contract have been enumerated in a contract which you signed, i.e., it must state among other things what the interest rate is going to be. If the interest rate changes, you must sign a new contract with the new terms on it. If you are to be charged a late fee, the contract you sign must state that you will be charged a late fee, how much that fee will be, and it must also state when and under what circumstances you will be charged a late fee. This contract must be signed by you and by the credit card company. Never happens.

However, when it comes time for the credit card companies and/or the collection agencies to sue you, they sue you based on your failure to live up to a contract.

Credit Card Companies try to get around this by sending out "notices" of changes in your interest rate, or changes in the amount of the late fees etc. Most of the time these "notices" are merely slick "stuffings" that are included with your credit card bill in print too tiny to be read by a normal person, and included with advertisements. Most people don't even know they are not advertisements. At any rate, changing the interest rate constitutes a new "contract" and you need to renegotiate this contract. But there was never a real contract to begin with!

You accepted a piece of plastic that gave you the

option of using someone else's money to buy something. You didn't sign a contract that said you would pay them back for it. Well, that's a bit of a simplification, but that's how I like to look at it.

That was just one of my arguments.

Somewhere in the back of my mind, I had the idea that if the question of credit card "agreements" being unconscionable contracts went to the State Appeals Court, new law might be written, which would in turn rein in some of the actions of the credit card companies, with their late fees, over-limit fees, and harassment.

Apparently the attorneys who filed the lawsuits against me were reading my mind, and didn't want the question to go to the Appeals Court. They didn't want to take that chance. I think they saw the logic in the argument, and they also saw that credit card "agreements" were, indeed, unconscionable contracts.

Unconscionable Contract   by Jana Lynn Shellman

WHAT IS AN UNCONSCIONABLE CONTRACT?

unconscionable adj. referring to a contract or bargain which is so unfair to a party that *no reasonable or informed person would agree to it.* In a suit for breach of contract, a court will not enforce an unconscionable contract (award damages or order specific performance) against the person unfairly treated on the theory that he/she was misled, lacked information, or signed under duress or misunderstanding. It is similar to an "adhesion contract," in which one party has taken advantage of a person dealing from weakness.

If you knew that the credit card company would have the ability to change the amount of the interest rate at will, without your written consent, would you have applied for it?

If you knew that the credit card company could change the date the payments came due at will, without your written consent, would you have applied for it?

33

If you knew that the credit card company could arbitrarily charge you exorbitant charges because their accounting department "had piles of payments that hadn't been credited to their accounts yet because of a computer breakdown" without your written consent would you have applied for it?

If you knew that you could be charged late fees and over-limit fees that increased during the time of the "contract" without your written permission, would you have applied for credit with that company?

It is my contention first and foremost that a credit card application is not a legal contract. It doesn't have the signature of anyone on it!   It does not have the elements of a contract. The credit card company changes the terms arbitrarily and constantly without getting your written consent to the changes. The credit card company invents new terms as it goes along, changing the conditions. The only notice "you get" is in the slick inserts that arrive in your bill along with other advertisements. They are too tiny to read and they get thrown out with the rest of the trash.

WHAT I DID WHEN THEY BEGAN SUING ME

The first thing I did was panic. For about ten seconds. And then I read the complaint. I looked for a copy of the "evidence" they claimed was attached to the complaint. There wasn't any! That kick-started me into my paralegal writing mode, and I began formulating my Answer in my head.   The more I thought about everything, the more I wrote. I considered all of my answers to their complaints, and then I began thinking of my Affirmative Defenses.   As I considered my Affirmative Defenses, I began formulating my Counterclaim against them.

Keep in mind that I'm not a lawyer, and you should not use these forms for yourself without first speaking to a lawyer to see if they apply to your situation, and/or the laws of your State.

THE PLEADINGS

Here's a copy of one of my Answers.

ANSWER & COUNTERCLAIM

COMES NOW the Defendant in person, and by way of Answer and Counterclaim to Plaintiff's Complaint would show this Honorable Court as follows:

That the Defendant denies the allegations contained in paragraphs 2, 3, and 4 of Plaintiff's complaint.

COUNTERCLAIM AND AFFIRMATIVE DEFENSES

COMES NOW the Defendant, and by way of counterclaim and Affirmative Defenses against the

Plaintiff would respectfully show this Honorable Court as follows:

That there was no Exhibit A attached to the Complaint which was received by first class mail and not properly served by the Sheriff by leaving or otherwise, and

That the Defendant was not properly served with an original of the Complaint, but received a copy of the complaint by regular U.S. Mail, which did not contain a copy of Exhibit "A" to the Defendant.

That the Defendant was forced to answer in a timely manner and was required to go to the Court House to look for the file and read the Exhibit "A" .

That the Court record showed Sheriff's service by leaving, which is contrary to the facts; and that

That the Defendant has never had a contract with the plaintiff.

That the Defendant has no clue as to who [collection agency] is collecting for, but that the Defendant does have a claim against [collection agency] for unfair collection practices in violation of the Fair Debt Collection Practices Act.

That the Plaintiff [collection agency] continued to make telephone calls to the Defendant after [collection agency] had been advised in writing to desist from such practices, and that the Defendant has witnesses to this fact, and in fact that in another case [collection agency] was forced to pay to the Defendant the sum of $80.00 for violation of this act.

That the Defendant has no idea who the Plaintiff is alleging that she owes $15,689.50 for a credit card debt That the Defendant has never owed any credit card company such an amount.

That the Defendant reserves the right to file an amended complaint, when and if the Plaintiff can supply proof of any charges made by the Defendant, copies of statements showing such billing, copies of a signed contract, or any proof that such a debt exists, other than the mysterious and nebulous claim of "arising out of the use of a credit card" description in the complaint.

That the Defendant's counterclaim against [collection agency] for the harassment and violation of Fair Debt Collection Practices Act is made here.

AFFIRMATIVE DEFENSES

COMES NOW the Defendant and counter claimant and by way of Counterclaim and Affirmative Defenses would respectfully show this Honorable Court as follows:

FRAUD AND CONCEALMENT: The Defendant

presents the affirmative defense of fraud, in that the original credit card issuer of whom Plaintiff, [collection agency] has taken the place fraudulently induced the Defendant to go further and further into debt by increasing the credit limit every time she paid off the debt, increasing the debt to its final limit, and the original creditor promised low interests rates, and when the Defendant no longer made payments because of her inability to work and earn a living, the original creditor increased the interest rate, added interest upon interest and added extraordinary and illegal charges, including but not limited to late charges in an amount which is contrary to Indiana statutes, making it impossible for the Defendant to extricate herself from the debt once she was ever again able to work.

That the original creditor concealed the change in

interest rate in vague language printed on the backs of inserts which may or may not have been legible without a magnifying glass, and which may or may not have been included in mailings to the Defendant, but if they were so included were disguised as "slick" junk mail inserts which ordinary and busy people routinely discard without reading.

That the elements of a contract are missing in that there was no acknowledgment of the terms of the contract by the debtor, no signature on any such change of terms, and notice was nefarious and/or nebulous to say the least.

That the original creditor was aware that debtors routinely discard such inserts (notices) without reading them, and that it was their pattern and practice to disguise such changes to their interest rates and other terms and conditions by presenting them in the fashion above-described, believing that in this matter they could avoid the legalities of providing the proper elements of a contract.

That the aforementioned practices should be challenged and forbidden as being treacherous and/or deceitful.

ILLEGALITY: That Defendant Counter-claimant presents the affirmative defense of illegality in that the original creditor increased any amounts owed by Defendant with illegal charges; that statutes of the State of Indiana dictate that late fee charges may only be in the total amount of $5.00 per month, and that the Defendant was consistently charged $20.00 or more per month for late fee charges.

ILLEGALITY: That the Plaintiff, [collection agency], its agents and employees, in its collection practices has violated the Fair Debt Collection Practices Act, in that telephone calls were made to the Defendant demanding payments prior to 8:00 A.M. Eastern Standard Time and after 9:00 P.M. Eastern Standard Time.

That although the Defendant has repeatedly written to [collection agency] and informed them they are never to call the Defendant for any purposes of collecting, that [collection agency] and its agents, attorneys and employees have telephoned the Defendant repeatedly over a period of many years, all contrary to the Fair Debt Collection Practices Act.

MITIGATION OF DAMAGES: That the Defendant has continuously written to all of her creditors attempting to make arrangements for settling this account, but that the original creditors have failed and refused to settle,

43

charges exorbitant interest charges and late fees. That although the Defendant has no idea who this creditor is, inasmuch as it has been turned over to [collection agency] it must surely be one of the debts that has not been settled to date.

PLAINTIFF NOT DULY LICENSED PURSUANT TO STATE LAW.   That the Plaintiff is not licensed as a creditor in the State of Indiana, or that the Plaintiff has failed and refused to present proof of such licensing.

UNCONSCIONABLE CONTRACT: That the original creditor induced the Defendant to enter into an unconscionable contract with the original creditor without providing the Defendant with a full and complete copy of the alleged contract, prior to the Defendant's signing of same; and that from the alleged institution of the account with the original creditor, the original creditor has continually made changes and added conditions to the alleged contract, all contrary to Indiana Law, and that no reasonable person would enter into such a contract without full knowledge of the conditions of the contract; and that the Defendant has never signed a full and complete contract, signing only an application for a credit card which contained none of the language of the contract.

WHEREFORE, the Defendant prays this Honorable Court find in her favor, that the Plaintiff take nothing by this complaint and that the Plaintiff be fined appropriately for its failure to abide by the statutes of the State of Indiana, and that the Plaintiff, [collection agency], be charged for Defendant's attorney fees, if any, for its failure to mitigate the damages and to arrange for the settling of this matter prior to suit, and at the time Defendant was able to make such arrangements for payment, and for such other and further relief as is just and proper in the premises.

WHAT HAPPENED NEXT?

After some time I got a copy of a Request for Extension of Time to Respond to my Answer and Counterclaims.

While I was waiting on their Response to my Answer, Affirmative Defenses, and Counterclaim, I sent off a Request for Production of Documents and Interrogatories. Here is a copy of one of those:

INTERROGATORIES AND REQUEST FOR PRODUCTION
OF DOCUMENTS PROPOUNDED TO PLAINTIFF

The Defendant respectfully requests the Plaintiff

to answer fully and under oath, within thirty-one (31)

days of receipt, the following interrogatories, and to

serve copies thereof upon counsel for the undersigned;

and to produce the documents and records requested

herein.

SCOPE AND NATURE OF INTERROGATORIES

These Interrogatories are continuing in nature and to the extent that information which cannot be obtained at the time of answer becomes known or available later, you are requested to furnish it as it becomes available.

These Interrogatories are directed to your personal knowledge, records and other information, and also the knowledge, records and other information of your attorneys, and any investigators, experts or any other representatives who have or who have had, an interest in the occurrence, and you are requested to obtain and furnish such information as you and/or they can obtain even though you do not presently have it recorded or separately noted.

REQUEST FOR PRODUCTION OF DOCUMENTS

Please produce copy of the contract allegedly signed by the Defendant with the Plaintiff.

Please produce copies of all records showing charges made to any accounts from the beginning of these accounts to date.

Please produce copies of the Defendant's signature upon such charges.

INTERROGATORIES

Please state the date the alleged contract was signed by the Defendant.

ANSWER:

Please state the total amount due and owing on October 2, 1997. [the date I notified all creditors of inability to pay].

ANSWER:

Please state the amount of the balance due on October 2, 1997 which was attributed to late charges and interest to that date.

ANSWER:

Please state the total amount of goods and/or services allegedly charged to these alleged accounts.

ANSWER:

Please state the total amount of interest added to these alleged accounts.

ANSWER:

Please state the total amount of late charges added to these alleged accounts.

ANSWER:

Please state the total amount of over-limit charges added to these alleged accounts.

ANSWER:

Please state the dates of any and all contracts in which these late charge fees and over-limit fees were mentioned, and provide copies which the Defendant signed in accordance with Indiana law.

AND THEN:

After some time I received a letter from the Attorney for the Plaintiff stating that none of the documents I had requested were available to the Plaintiff, and they could not send them to me. I also received another letter, almost simultaneously that said basically: "we give up."   And they sent the following instrument to which I added a couple of terms.

STIPULATION RESOLVING COMPLAINT & COUNTERCLAIM

COME NOW the parties, [collection agency] by its attorney, and [me], and hereby agree as follows:

On or about June of 2002, [collection agency] filed a complaint against Defendant for a sum it alleged due and owing from Defendant to [creditors].

On or about June 30, 2002, Defendant filed her Answer and Counterclaim against [collection agency].

Plaintiff and Defendant have since reached an agreement to mutually dismiss all of the claims each has against the other from the beginning of time to the present regarding the creation, servicing, and collection of said [creditors]..

The Defendant disputes the allegations contained in Plaintiff's complaint.

The Plaintiff disputes the allegations contained in the Defendant's counterclaim.

NOW, THEREFORE, IT IS HEREBY ORDERED: Plaintiff/Counter-Defendant and Defendant/Counter-Claimant hereby move to mutually dismiss with prejudice the complaint and counter-complaint simultaneously.

For good and valuable consideration, the receipt and adequacy of which is hereby acknowledged, Defendant hereby releases, discharges, and acquits [collection agency], [creditors], and each of their respective officers, directors, shareholders, agents (including collection agencies), employees, successors, predecessors and assigns of and from any and all Claims (as defined in the next sentence) related to the [creditors'] accounts. "Claims" shall be defined as any and all claims, debts, demands, defenses, actions, causes of action, suits, sums of money, warranties, covenants, contracts, controversies, promises, agreements or obligations, of any type or description and any other claim or demand of any nature whatsoever, whether existing by virtue of state, federal, bankruptcy or non-bankruptcy federal law that exists now or has ever existed as of this date, specifically including any claims that were raised or could have been raised in Defendant's counter-complaint. "Claims" specifically excludes Plaintiff's obligations under this Stipulation Resolving Complaint.

For good and valuable consideration, the receipt and adequacy of which is hereby acknowledged, [collection agency] hereby releases, discharges, and acquits [Me], and successors, predecessors and assigns of and from any and all Claims (as defined in the next sentence) related to the [creditors] accounts. "Claims" shall be defined as any and all claims, debts, demands, defenses, actions, causes of action, suits, sums of money, warranties, covenants, contracts, controversies, promises, agreements or obligations, of any type or description and any other claim or demand of any nature whatsoever, whether existing by virtue of state, federal, bankruptcy or non-bankruptcy federal law that exists now or has ever existed as of this date, specifically including any claims that were raised or could have been raised in Defendant's counter-complaint. "Claims" specifically excludes Defendant's obligations under this Stipulation Resolving Complaint.

Unconscionable Contract

by Jana Lynn Shellman

DOES THIS HELP YOUR CREDIT?

If you have gone a year without good credit, and with a lot of lawsuits, those things are going to show up on your credit rating. You're probably not going to have good credit. I don't know. I haven't tried to get credit for anything.

I was never late on my mortgage payment, and have made those payments consistently from the time I got the mortgage in 1991 until the present.

I also requested that the Credit Reporting Agencies be advised that these accounts were settled, that they were NOT written off, but settled equally, and that no report to the state or federal taxation agencies were to be made, as we had agreed that I had not profited from this stipulation, but that we had both broken even.

At the present time my credit rating is over 700 but I haven't tried to get a loan anywhere. It's been more than ten years since these were dismissed.

<u>Unconscionable Contract</u>　　　　　　　by Jana Lynn Shellman

<u>HOW DO YOU LIVE WITHOUT CREDIT CARDS?</u>

It's relatively easy.   You make sure you have a savings account, and a checking account, and then you get debit cards from your bank or credit union.   Then you don't use them unless you have the money in the bank to cover your usage.

You have to plan ahead. And you have to keep good records. I do all of my record keeping by doing my banking on line.

I have access to all of my accounts on my smart phone and I have a good communication with my bank and my credit union. If I am out and want to make a major purchase with my card (and I do use it as a credit card, with the knowledge that the money will be taken immediately from my account), I call the bank or credit union and ask them to make the transfer from my savings to my checking when I know there's not enough in the checking side.   I could do this on my smart phone as well, but for larger amounts I'd rather do it by talking to a human being and making sure they do the transfer. Then I check it on my smart phone, by going to my accounts and making sure it shows.

You only need to do this for a major purchase where you've used the card for a big purchase. For smaller purchases, I just always make sure there's enough on the checking side before I go shopping. I've used the debit cards for airline flights, car rentals, hotels, and purchases while I'm traveling. Sometimes you'll get a call from them wanting to know if you're really in Timbuktu and making those purchases. It's a bit annoying when you're traveling, but it's also somewhat reassuring to know they are checking to make sure it's really you spending all your money.

WHAT IF YOU HAVE TO FILE BANKRUPTCY?

_____In 2004, I was once again working for an attorney, and I ended up in the hospital with heart problems. I had to have a triple bypass. I didn't have health insurance. However, even if I had health insurance, I would still have had to file for bankruptcy because the medical and hospital bills amounted to close to $185,000.00. My co-pay would have amounted to more than $20,000.00. I didn't have a choice but to file bankruptcy. Don't think I didn't examine every creative possibility otherwise, but it just wasn't there. I had a choice to turn my house (after it was paid for) over to the State and have Medicaid pay my bill, or to file bankruptcy.

I carefully examined the Medicaid paperwork and it was incredibly intrusive. It wanted to know things about me I felt were not the business of the State.

For that reason, I sat down and prepared my own bankruptcy. I had already been preparing documentation for others to file bankruptcy, and I had the software to do it.

I held off on filing, however, until I had exhausted

all of my savings. At that time, all I had was a small 401K that had accumulated once I'd gone back to work after 1997 that amounted to about $3,000.00. I saved back just enough of it to pay my bankruptcy filing fee. I was working from home during my recovery, but not making a lot of money. At that time the filing fee was almost more than I could come up with.

I kept my house because the equity was less than $7500.00, which at that time was the amount of the exemption for a single person. I kept my car because it's old enough to vote! With the exemptions that are available, you can keep most of your furniture and furnishings, and the like. If you have valuable assets, however, such as rare paintings, books, and the like, you won't be able to keep them. They are not exempt.

If you choose to be your own representative in bankruptcy court, I'd advise being doubly careful to follow all the rules, and not attempt to hide any of your assets. Don't forget anything! I've known people who went to prison for "forgetting" certain assets, or trying to hide their assets from the bankruptcy court.

As a legal note, when I do prepare bankruptcy documentation for others, I recommend that they first go to see a bankruptcy attorney, ask the attorney all the questions they need to know about filing for bankruptcy, and find out whether or not they can afford to hire an attorney to file the bankruptcy.   If after this interview with the attorney the person feels they still cannot afford to pay an attorney to prepare the documentation and appear in bankruptcy Court with them, then I give them a questionnaire that asks all of the questions for which answers will be needed in the preparation of the documentation, I tell them it is their responsibility to make sure they have made me a list of all of their creditors, with the names and addresses of all of them, the approximate date the debt was incurred and if it has been assigned to a debt collector as well. Then I also have them prepare a list of all of their assets and the location of the same. I give them a document to sign that says they understand I cannot give them any legal advice, and that all I can do is prepare the documentation based upon the information they have given to me, and that they are fully responsible for everything going into the documentation, and they will not have an attorney with them in Court. I charge them a document preparation fee that is approximately 10%-20% of what the attorney would charge.   Anyone can prepare their own bankruptcy forms for filing by going to the local bankruptcy clerk and requesting the information. At one time forms for filing bankruptcy were available in stationery stores. I'm not certain whether they are still available or not. I do know that the forms are available on line (the link follows in the next chapter.)

There is a provision in Bankruptcy Court for non-attorney document preparers to prepare your bankruptcy papers for you. They must fill out a form and submit it to the Court showing that they prepared the paperwork.

There are non-attorney bankruptcy document preparers all over the country. If you look for them you will probably find them. You could ask at the local bankruptcy clerk's office for names of non-attorneys who prepare bankruptcy documents. I'm not certain they will give you those names, but they may do so. I know I, as a non-attorney, considered advertising that I could do document preparation for bankruptcy filings, and various advertising media thought it would be a bad idea, i.e., practicing law without a license, if I were to do so. Just to be on the safe side, I don't advertise.

BANKRUPTCY COURT INFORMATION

B a n k r u p t c y   F o r m s :
http://www.uscourts.gov/FormsAndFees/Forms/Bankr
uptcyForms.aspx

The following information was obtained from the Bankruptcy Court web site:

CHAPTER 7:

Liquidation Under the Bankruptcy Code

The chapter of the Bankruptcy Code providing for "liquidation," (i.e., the sale of a debtor's nonexempt property and the distribution of the proceeds to creditors.)

Alternatives to Chapter 7

Debtors should be aware that there are several alternatives to chapter 7 relief. For example, debtors who are engaged in business, including corporations, partnerships, and sole proprietorships, may prefer to remain in business and avoid liquidation. Such debtors should consider filing a petition under chapter 11 of the Bankruptcy Code. Under chapter 11, the debtor may seek an adjustment of debts, either by reducing the debt or by extending the time for repayment, or may seek a more comprehensive reorganization. Sole proprietorships may also be eligible for relief under chapter 13 of the Bankruptcy Code.

In addition, individual debtors who have regular income may seek an adjustment of debts under chapter 13 of the Bankruptcy Code. A particular advantage of chapter 13 is that it provides individual debtors with an opportunity to save their homes from foreclosure by allowing them to "catch up" past due payments through a payment plan. Moreover, the court may dismiss a chapter 7 case filed by an individual whose debts are primarily consumer rather than business debts if the court finds that the granting of relief would be an abuse of chapter 7. 11 U.S.C. § 707(b).

If the debtor's "current monthly income" (1) is more than the state median, the Bankruptcy Code requires application of a "means test" to determine whether the chapter 7 filing is presumptively abusive. Abuse is presumed if the debtor's aggregate current monthly income over 5 years, net of certain statutorily allowed expenses, is more than (i) $11,725, or (ii) 25%

of the debtor's nonpriority unsecured debt, as long as that amount is at least $7,025. (2) The debtor may rebut a presumption of abuse only by a showing of special circumstances that justify additional expenses or adjustments of current monthly income. Unless the debtor overcomes the presumption of abuse, the case will generally be converted to chapter 13 (with the debtor's consent) or will be dismissed. 11 U.S.C. § 707(b)(1).

Debtors should also be aware that out-of-court agreements with creditors or debt counseling services may provide an alternative to a bankruptcy filing.

Background

A chapter 7 bankruptcy case does not involve the filing of a plan of repayment as in chapter 13. Instead, the bankruptcy trustee gathers and sells the debtor's nonexempt assets and uses the proceeds of such assets to pay holders of claims (creditors) in accordance with the provisions of the Bankruptcy Code. Part of the debtor's property may be subject to liens and mortgages that pledge the property to other creditors. In addition, the Bankruptcy Code will allow the debtor to keep certain "exempt" property; but a trustee will liquidate the debtor's remaining assets. Accordingly, potential debtors should realize that the filing of a petition under chapter 7 may result in the loss of property.

Chapter 7 Eligibility

To qualify for relief under chapter 7 of the Bankruptcy Code, the debtor may be an individual, a partnership, or a corporation or other business entity. 11 U.S.C. §§ 101(41), 109(b). Subject to the means test described above for individual debtors, relief is available under chapter 7 irrespective of the amount of the debtor's debts or whether the debtor is solvent or insolvent. An individual cannot file under chapter 7 or any other chapter, however, if during the preceding 180 days a prior bankruptcy petition was dismissed due to the debtor's willful failure to appear before the court or comply with orders of the court, or the debtor voluntarily dismissed the previous case after creditors sought relief from the bankruptcy court to recover property upon which they hold liens. 11 U.S.C. §§ 109(g), 362(d) and (e). In addition, no individual may be a debtor under chapter 7 or any chapter of the Bankruptcy Code unless he or she has, within 180 days before filing, received credit counseling from an approved credit counseling agency either in an individual or group briefing. 11 U.S.C. §§ 109, 111. There are exceptions in emergency situations or where the U.S. trustee (or bankruptcy administrator) has determined that there are insufficient approved agencies to provide the required counseling. If a debt management plan is developed during required credit counseling, it must be filed with the court.

One of the primary purposes of bankruptcy is to discharge certain debts to give an honest individual debtor a "fresh start." The debtor has no liability for discharged debts. In a chapter 7 case, however, a discharge is only available to individual debtors, not to partnerships or corporations. 11 U.S.C. § 727(a)(1). Although an individual chapter 7 case usually results in a discharge of debts, the right to a discharge is not absolute, and some types of debts are not discharged. Moreover, a bankruptcy discharge does not extinguish a lien on property.

How Chapter 7 Works

A chapter 7 case begins with the debtor filing a petition with the bankruptcy court serving the area where the individual lives or where the business debtor is organized or has its principal place of business or principal assets. (3) In addition to the petition, the debtor must also file with the court: (1) schedules of assets and liabilities; (2) a schedule of current income and expenditures; (3) a statement of financial affairs; and (4) a schedule of executory contracts and unexpired leases. Fed. R. Bankr. P. 1007(b). Debtors must also provide the assigned case trustee with a copy of the tax return or transcripts for the most recent tax year as well as tax returns filed during the case (including tax returns for prior years that had not been filed when the case began). 11 U.S.C. § 521. Individual debtors with primarily consumer debts have additional document filing requirements. They must file: a certificate of credit counseling and a copy of any debt repayment plan developed through credit counseling; evidence of payment from employers, if any, received 60 days before filing; a statement of monthly net income and any anticipated increase in income or expenses after filing; and a record of any interest the debtor has in federal or state qualified education or tuition accounts. Id. A husband and wife may file a joint petition or individual petitions. 11 U.S.C. § 302(a). Even if filing jointly, a husband and wife are subject to all the document filing requirements of individual debtors. (The Official Forms may be purchased at legal stationery stores or downloaded from the internet at www.uscourts.gov/bkforms/index.html. They are not available from the court.)

FEES:

The courts must charge a $245 case filing fee, a $39 miscellaneous administrative fee, and a $15 trustee surcharge. Normally, the fees must be paid to the clerk of the court upon filing. With the court's permission, however, individual debtors may pay in installments. 28 U.S.C. § 1930(a); Fed. R. Bankr. P. 1006(b); Bankruptcy Court Miscellaneous Fee Schedule, Item 8. The number of installments is limited to four, and the debtor must make the final installment no later than 120 days after filing the petition. Fed. R. Bankr. P. 1006. For cause shown, the court may extend the time of any installment, provided that the last installment is paid not later than 180 days after filing the petition. Id. The debtor may also pay the $39 administrative fee and the $15 trustee surcharge in installments. If a joint petition is filed, only one filing fee, one administrative fee, and one trustee surcharge are charged. Debtors should be aware that failure to pay these fees may result in dismissal of the case. 11 U.S.C. § 707(a).

If the debtor's income is less than 150% of the poverty level (as defined in the Bankruptcy Code), and the debtor is unable to pay the chapter 7 fees even in

71

installments, the court may waive the requirement that the fees be paid. 28 U.S.C. § 1930(f).

WHAT YOU'LL NEED TO FILE:

In order to complete the Official Bankruptcy Forms that make up the petition, statement of financial affairs, and schedules, the debtor must provide the following information:

A list of all creditors and the amount and nature of their claims;

The source, amount, and frequency of the debtor's income;

A list of all of the debtor's property; and

A detailed list of the debtor's monthly living expenses, i.e., food, clothing, shelter, utilities, taxes, transportation, medicine, etc.

Married individuals must gather this information for their spouse regardless of whether they are filing a joint petition, separate individual petitions, or even if only one spouse is filing. In a situation where only one spouse files, the income and expenses of the non-filing spouse are required so that the court, the trustee and creditors can evaluate the household's financial position.

Among the schedules that an individual debtor will file is a schedule of "exempt" property. The Bankruptcy Code allows an individual debtor (4) to protect some property from the claims of creditors

73

because it is exempt under federal bankruptcy law or under the laws of the debtor's home state. 11 U.S.C. § 522(b). Many states have taken advantage of a provision in the Bankruptcy Code that permits each state to adopt its own exemption law in place of the federal exemptions. In other jurisdictions, the individual debtor has the option of choosing between a federal package of exemptions or the exemptions available under state law. Thus, whether certain property is exempt and may be kept by the debtor is often a question of state law. The debtor should consult an attorney to determine the exemptions available in the state where the debtor lives.

Filing a petition under chapter 7 "automatically stays" (stops) most collection actions against the debtor or the debtor's property. 11 U.S.C. § 362. But filing the petition does not stay certain types of actions listed under 11 U.S.C. § 362(b), and the stay may be effective only for a short time in some situations. The stay arises by operation of law and requires no judicial action. As long as the stay is in effect, creditors generally may not initiate or continue lawsuits, wage garnishments, or even telephone calls demanding payments. The bankruptcy clerk gives notice of the bankruptcy case to all creditors whose names and addresses are provided by the debtor.

Between 20 and 40 days after the petition is filed, the case trustee (described below) will hold a meeting of creditors. If the U.S. trustee or bankruptcy administrator (5) schedules the meeting at a place that does not have regular U.S. trustee or bankruptcy administrator staffing, the meeting may be held no more than 60 days after the order for relief. Fed. R. Bankr. P. 2003(a). During this meeting, the trustee puts the debtor under oath, and both the trustee and creditors may ask questions. The debtor must attend the meeting and answer questions regarding the debtor's financial affairs and property. 11 U.S.C. § 343. If a husband and wife have filed a joint petition, they both must attend the creditors' meeting and answer questions. Within 10 days of the creditors' meeting, the U.S. trustee will report to the court whether the case should be presumed to be an abuse under the means test described in 11 U.S.C. § 704(b).

It is important for the debtor to cooperate with the trustee and to provide any financial records or documents that the trustee requests. The Bankruptcy Code requires the trustee to ask the debtor questions at the meeting of creditors to ensure that the debtor is aware of the potential consequences of seeking a discharge in bankruptcy such as the effect on credit history, the ability to file a petition under a different chapter, the effect of receiving a discharge, and the effect of reaffirming a debt. Some trustees provide written information on these topics at or before the meeting to ensure that the debtor is aware of this information. In order to preserve their independent judgment, bankruptcy judges are prohibited from attending the meeting of creditors. 11 U.S.C. § 341(c). In order to accord the debtor complete relief, the Bankruptcy Code allows the debtor to convert a chapter 7 case to a case under chapter 11, 12, or 13 (6) as long as the debtor is eligible to be a debtor under the new chapter. However, a condition of the debtor's voluntary conversion is that the case has not previously been converted to chapter 7 from another chapter. 11 U.S.C. § 706(a). Thus, the debtor will not be permitted to convert the case repeatedly from one chapter to another.

Role of the Case Trustee

When a chapter 7 petition is filed, the U.S. trustee (or the bankruptcy court in Alabama and North Carolina) appoints an impartial case trustee to administer the case and liquidate the debtor's nonexempt assets. 11 U.S.C. §§ 701, 704. If all the debtor's assets are exempt or subject to valid liens, the trustee will normally file a "no asset" report with the court, and there will be no distribution to unsecured creditors. Most chapter 7 cases involving individual debtors are no asset cases. But if the case appears to be an "asset" case at the outset, unsecured creditors (7) must file their claims with the court within 90 days after the first date set for the meeting of creditors. Fed. R. Bankr. P. 3002(c). A governmental unit, however, has 180 days from the date the case is filed to file a claim. 11 U.S.C. § 502(b)(9). In the typical no asset chapter 7 case, there is no need for creditors to file proofs of claim because there will be no distribution. If the trustee later recovers assets for distribution to unsecured creditors, the Bankruptcy Court will provide notice to creditors and will allow additional time to file proofs of claim. Although a secured creditor does not need to file a proof of claim in a chapter 7 case to preserve its security interest or lien, there may be other reasons to file a claim. A creditor in a chapter 7 case who has a lien on the debtor's property should consult an attorney for advice.

Commencement of a bankruptcy case creates an "estate." The estate technically becomes the temporary legal owner of all the debtor's property. It consists of all legal or equitable interests of the debtor in property as of the commencement of the case, including property owned or held by another person if the debtor has an interest in the property. Generally speaking, the debtor's creditors are paid from nonexempt property of the estate.

The primary role of a chapter 7 trustee in an asset case is to liquidate the debtor's nonexempt assets in a manner that maximizes the return to the debtor's unsecured creditors. The trustee accomplishes this by selling the debtor's property if it is free and clear of liens (as long as the property is not exempt) or if it is worth more than any security interest or lien attached to the property and any exemption that the debtor holds in the property. The trustee may also attempt to recover money or property under the trustee's "avoiding powers." The trustee's avoiding powers include the power to: set aside preferential transfers made to creditors within 90 days before the petition; undo security interests and other prepetition transfers of property that were not properly perfected under nonbankruptcy law at the time of the petition; and pursue nonbankruptcy claims such as fraudulent conveyance and bulk transfer remedies available under state law. In addition, if the debtor is a business, the bankruptcy court may authorize the trustee to operate the business for a limited period of time, if such operation will benefit creditors and enhance the liquidation of the estate. 11 U.S.C. § 721.

Section 726 of the Bankruptcy Code governs the distribution of the property of the estate. Under § 726, there are six classes of claims; and each class must be paid in full before the next lower class is paid anything. The debtor is only paid if all other classes of claims have been paid in full. Accordingly, the debtor is not particularly interested in the trustee's disposition of the estate assets, except with respect to the payment of those debts which for some reason are not dischargeable in the bankruptcy case. The individual debtor's primary concerns in a chapter 7 case are to retain exempt property and to receive a discharge that covers as many debts as possible.

The Chapter 7 Discharge

A discharge releases individual debtors from personal liability for most debts and prevents the creditors owed those debts from taking any collection actions against the debtor. Because a chapter 7 discharge is subject to many exceptions, debtors should consult competent legal counsel before filing to discuss the scope of the discharge. Generally, excluding cases that are dismissed or converted, individual debtors receive a discharge in more than 99 percent of chapter 7 cases. In most cases, unless a party in interest files a complaint objecting to the discharge or a motion to extend the time to object, the bankruptcy court will issue a discharge order relatively early in the case – generally, 60 to 90 days after the date first set for the meeting of creditors. Fed. R. Bankr. P. 4004(c).

The grounds for denying an individual debtor a discharge in a chapter 7 case are narrow and are construed against the moving party. Among other reasons, the court may deny the debtor a discharge if it finds that the debtor: failed to keep or produce adequate books or financial records; failed to explain satisfactorily any loss of assets; committed a bankruptcy crime such as perjury; failed to obey a lawful order of the bankruptcy court; fraudulently transferred, concealed, or destroyed property that would have become property of the estate; or failed to complete an approved instructional course concerning financial management. 11 U.S.C. § 727; Fed. R. Bankr. P. 4005. Secured creditors may retain some rights to seize property securing an underlying debt even after a discharge is granted. Depending on individual circumstances, if a debtor wishes to keep certain secured property (such as an automobile), he or she may decide to "reaffirm" the debt. A reaffirmation is an agreement between the debtor and the creditor that the debtor will remain liable and will pay all or a portion of the money owed, even though the debt would otherwise be discharged in the bankruptcy. In return, the creditor promises that it will not repossess or take back the automobile or other property so long as the debtor continues to pay the debt.

If the debtor decides to reaffirm a debt, he or she must do so before the discharge is entered. The debtor must sign a written reaffirmation agreement and file it with the court. 11 U.S.C. § 524(c). The Bankruptcy Code requires that reaffirmation agreements contain an extensive set of disclosures described in 11 U.S.C. § 524(k). Among other things, the disclosures must advise the debtor of the amount of the debt being reaffirmed and how it is calculated and that reaffirmation means that the debtor's personal liability for that debt will not be discharged in the bankruptcy. The disclosures also require the debtor to sign and file a statement of his or her current income and expenses which shows that the balance of income paying expenses is sufficient to pay the reaffirmed debt. If the balance is not enough to pay the debt to be reaffirmed, there is a presumption of undue hardship, and the court may decide not to approve the reaffirmation agreement. Unless the debtor is represented by an attorney, the bankruptcy judge must approve the reaffirmation agreement.

If the debtor was represented by an attorney in connection with the reaffirmation agreement, the attorney must certify in writing that he or she advised the debtor of the legal effect and consequences of the agreement, including a default under the agreement. The attorney must also certify that the debtor was fully informed and voluntarily made the agreement and that reaffirmation of the debt will not create an undue hardship for the debtor or the debtor's dependants. 11 U.S.C. § 524(k). The Bankruptcy Code requires a reaffirmation hearing if the debtor has not been represented by an attorney during the negotiating of the agreement, or if the court disapproves the reaffirmation agreement. 11 U.S.C. § 524(d) and (m). The debtor may repay any debt voluntarily, however, whether or not a reaffirmation agreement exists. 11 U.S.C. § 524(f). An individual receives a discharge for most of his or her debts in a chapter 7 bankruptcy case. A creditor may no longer initiate or continue any legal or other action against the debtor to collect a discharged debt. But not all of an individual's debts are discharged in chapter 7. Debts not discharged include debts for alimony and child support, certain taxes, debts for certain educational benefit overpayments or loans made or guaranteed by a governmental unit, debts for willful and malicious injury by the debtor to another entity or to the property of another entity, debts for death or personal injury caused by the debtor's operation of a motor vehicle while the debtor was intoxicated from alcohol or other substances, and debts for certain criminal restitution orders. 11 U.S.C. § 523(a). The debtor will continue to be liable for these types of debts to the extent that they are not paid in the chapter 7 case. Debts for money or property obtained by false pretenses, debts for fraud or defalcation while acting in a fiduciary capacity, and debts for willful and malicious injury by the debtor to another entity or to the property of another entity will be discharged unless a creditor timely files and prevails in an action to have such debts declared non-dischargeable. 11 U.S.C. § 523(c); Fed. R. Bankr. P. 4007(c).

The court may revoke a chapter 7 discharge on the request of the trustee, a creditor, or the U.S. trustee if the discharge was obtained through fraud by the debtor, if the debtor acquired property that is property of the estate and knowingly and fraudulently failed to report the acquisition of such property or to surrender the property to the trustee, or if the debtor (without a satisfactory explanation) makes a material misstatement or fails to provide documents or other information in connection with an audit of the debtor's case. 11 U.S.C. § 727(d).

NOTES

The "current monthly income" received by the debtor is a defined term in the Bankruptcy Code and means the average monthly income received over the six calendar months before commencement of the bankruptcy case, including regular contributions to household expenses from nondebtors and including income from the debtor's spouse if the petition is a joint petition, but not including social security income or certain payments made because the debtor is the victim of certain crimes. 11 U.S.C. § 101(10A).

To determine whether a presumption of abuse arises, all individual debtors with primarily consumer debts who file a chapter 7 case must complete Official Bankruptcy Form B22A, entitled "Statement of Current Monthly Income and Means Test Calculation - For Use in Chapter 7." (The Official Forms may be purchased at legal stationery stores or downloaded from the internet at www.uscourts.gov/bkforms/index.html . They are not available from the court.)

An involuntary chapter 7 case may be commenced under certain circumstances by a petition filed by creditors holding claims against the debtor. 11 U.S.C. § 303.

Each debtor in a joint case (both husband and wife) can claim exemptions under the federal bankruptcy laws. 11 U.S.C. § 522(m).

In North Carolina and Alabama, bankruptcy administrators perform similar functions that U.S. trustees perform in the remaining 48 states. These duties include establishing a panel of private trustees to serve as trustees in chapter 7 cases and supervising the administration of cases and trustees in cases under chapters 7, 11, 12, and 13 of the Bankruptcy Code. The bankruptcy administrator program is administered by the Administrative Office of the United States Courts, while the U.S. trustee program is administered by the Department of Justice. For purposes of this publication, references to U.S. trustees are also applicable to bankruptcy administrators.

A fee is charged for converting, on request of the debtor, a case under chapter 7 to a case under chapter

11. The fee charged is the difference between the filing fee for a chapter 7 and the filing fee for a chapter 11. 28 U.S.C. § 1930(a). Currently, the difference is $755. Id. There is no fee for converting from chapter 7 to chapter 13.

Unsecured debts generally may be defined as those for which the extension of credit was based purely upon an evaluation by the creditor of the debtor's ability to pay, as opposed to secured debts, for which the extension of credit was based upon the creditor's right to seize collateral on default, in addition to the debtor's ability to pay.

Acessing Legal Resources:

The following link should take you top a source for further information:

http://www.uscourts.gov/FederalCourts/Bankruptcy/BankruptcyResources.aspx

Business Credit Cards

Like me, you may have suddenly begun receiving "business" credit card application announcements in the mail. I always threw them away, wondering why they would send them to me. The following is an interesting article I found by Sheryl Nance-Nash in this regard.

Beware of Business Credit Cards: A Consumer Protection Loophole
By Sheryl Nance-Nash

"When the Obama administration and Democrats in Congress enacted the Credit CARD Act of 2009, the goal was to make credit cards safer and their rules more transparent for everybody. But leave it to banks to find the loopholes. Those new consumer protections weren't extended to cards designated for business or commercial use, and as a result, millions of American households are at risk from business credit cards, warns the Pew Health Group's Safe Credit Cards Project.

"According to Pew, 40 years ago, business credit cards

were excluded from federal consumer protections because policymakers concluded that business owners were in a position to analyze their risks. But banks are casting a very wide net in their search for new "business" customers. Between January 2006 and December 2010, American households received more than 2.6 billion mailed offers for business credit cards, Pew found. And whether the recipient was a large company, the owner of a small company, or just an employee, they're personally liable for all charges -- and again, they aren't protected by the key provisions in the Credit CARD Act.

"As a result, practices that federal regulators deemed "unfair" or "deceptive," such as hair-trigger interest rate hikes and unpredictable rate increases, remain widespread for business credit cards that are regularly offered to American households.

"Every month, more than 10 million business credit card offers are mailed to households at all income levels. The sheer number of offers that are sent to homes all across the nation represents a risk to millions of American families," said Nick Bourke, director of Pew's

Safe Credit Cards Project, in a prepared statement.

You Don't Have to Be a Business

"There are all sorts of ways people end up on a mailing list to receive a business credit card solicitation. If you're are a doctor, lawyer, or other professional, issuers may guess that you might have your own business. Sometimes, they rely on demographics: If your neighborhood is home to entrepreneurs, you could get put into that category by association, Bourke explained to DailyFinance, an online information site you might want to visit.

"While the total number of individuals who actually hold business credit cards is unclear, there are at least 11 million "small business" credit card accounts, with an average of 1.4 cards per account, according to Pew's research.

"To better protect individuals, families and small business owners, we urge that the safeguards found in the Credit CARD Act be extended to any card on which the cardholder is personally liable," says Pew.

Boosting Their Profits Any Way They Can

"The report's findings show that banks are pretty much doing whatever they want when it comes to business credit cards.

"For example, 80% of business card accounts had an "any time change in terms" clause with no right to opt out, which means that the banks can change the account terms with little or no notice. By contrast, under the CARD Act, terms on consumer cards cannot change during the first year; after that, 45 days notice is required, and consumers generally may opt out of the changes. Existing balances are also protected from arbitrary rate increases.

"Further, 67% of business card contracts stipulated penalty interest rates for late payments or over-limit transactions. Issuers can apply penalty rates immediately and without notice for any violation, and those high rates can last indefinitely on any balance. Under the CARD Act, penalty interest rates may not be applied to existing balances on consumer credit cards, unless an account is seriously delinquent.

"With business credit cards, penalty fees are virtually unrestricted and may not be reasonable and proportional to the violation. Late fees (median amount $39) can be assessed on 73% of business cards , while 67% were subject to over-limit fees (median amount $39).

"Again, contrast that to consumers credit cards, where users are protected because penalty fees must be "reasonable and proportional," -- generally $25 for the first and $35 for additional violations within six months. Fees must not exceed the violation, for example, the penalty for a $4 over-limit transaction must be $4 or less. And over-limit fees can't be charged unless the cardholder has opted in and said that the bank may allow such transactions to clear.

"Then too, issuers can direct payments on business cards first to low-rate balances, such as balance transfers, while interest accrues on higher-rate balances: 84% of business card disclosures gave issuers sole power to maximize finance charges by applying payments to low-rate balances first. For consumer cards, any payment amount above the monthly minimum must be applied to the highest-rate balance first, reducing interest charges to cardholders.

Bank of America and Capital One: The Good Guys?

"While there is plenty of shame to spread around, Pew's research also highlights the "good guys" -- issuers who have voluntarily applied portions of the Credit CARD Act to their business cards. Bank of America (BAC) eliminated penalty interest rates, over-limit fees and late fees and both Bank of America and Capital One (COF) have adopted application of payments to be applied to the larger balance first.

"The practices of these banks show that additional consumer protections can be applied to all credit cards marketed to American households and that issuers can still receive fair compensation for the service provided," said Bourke. "Now is the time for policymakers to ensure that the actions of these banks are not the exception, but rather the rule."

"At a minimum, Pew recommends that the government extend the consumer protections of the Credit CARD Act to any credit card product that requires an individual to be personally or jointly liable for account expenses.

"Also high on their to-do list: Require issuers to tell applicants whenever a credit card isn't covered by the Credit CARD Act. Moreover, account disclosures should warn of additional risks not found in their consumer credit cards.

"But for now, the moral is: Go to the mailbox at your own risk. Quite simply, said Bourke, "If you don't own a business, just use a normal consumer credit card. You will get better legal protection."

The foregoing information source accredited to Pew's Safe Credit Cards Project.

Unconscionable Contract   by Jana Lynn Shellman

HAVE THE LAWS CHANGED
SINCE I FILED AGAINST
THE CREDIT CARD COMPANIES

_____It isn't so much that the laws have changed, it is in the methods taken by attorneys to sue for collection of credit card debt. The cases that were filed against me were filed as complaints on contracts, which is why I could plead unconscionable contract as one of my defenses.

However, the laws have changed somewhat, but there are still unscrupulous collection agencies and collection agents who take advantage of our ignorance to bully us into making payments. They harass us and take advantage of us.

Nevertheless, it would be a good idea to understand the new law with regard to credit card usage:

The new credit card laws aren't completely in your best interest, and the credit card companies and the collection agencies are already working around the new laws.

I still don't think the credit card laws address the issue of a credit card purchase not being a contract and not having the elements of a contract, so in the collection process the litigators still cannot call an action for collection a default in contract.

The Federal Reserve Boards new credit card regulations are in force now, and new credit card laws have been phased in over the last year or so. The object was to protect us from predatory fees from credit card issuers.

Creditor Card issuers had about 9 months to prepare for the implementation of the new rules.

Many consumers have had their credit card accounts closed, interest rates increased and credit card limits reduced. That was leading up to the first phase of the new rules.

Following is a summary of the new rules:

The rules aren't that easy to understand. The Federal Reserve Board has given credit card companies some decision-making leeway on rate increases and account re-evaluations.

Credit card accounts that have had interest rates increased must be re-evaluated every 6 months and the interest rates lowered "if appropriate". They were pretty vague about what is appropriate.

These rules seem to apply only if you are paying your credit card on time, in the correct amount. Your check can't bounce and then if the credit card company thinks its appropriate your credit card rate might go lower.

That does not mean they'll put your interest rates back to the rate you had prior to the increase.

Credit Card Interest Rate
Increases Must be Explained

If your credit card issuer raises your interest rate they must tell you why, under the new rules from the Federal Reserve Board,

Your creditors must send a 45 day notice if they intend to:

- Increase your credit card interest rate
- Change fees associated with your credit card account, annual fees, late fees etc.
- Make changes to the terms on your credit card.

Exceptions to the 45-Day
Credit Card Change Notice:

If your credit card rate is tied to an index and the index goes up so will your cards rate.

Introductory credit card rates must be in force for at least 6 months.

After 6 months of the introductory rates, your credit card rates may be raised to whatever rate you agreed to.

If you have a workout agreement and are late, or miss a payment, your rates can go up.

If you are more than 60 days late your rates can go up.

Other Changes in the Law Now In Force:

Maximum Penalty fee is $25.00. Includes late fees or other agreement violations.

Exception: If you have repeated violations your

creditor can charge higher fees, but must justify them.

Credit Card Penalty fees cannot exceed the minimum payment required.

Credit Card Inactivity fees are banned.

Multiple fees stemming from a single violation are forbidden.

No Credit Card Interest Rate
Increased for the First Year.

Your creditor cannot increase your interest rates for the first year on a "new" account.

Here are the exceptions to the first year rate increase restriction:

If your credit card rate is tied to an index and the index goes up so will your cards rate.

Credit card introductory rates must be in force for at least 6 months.

After 6 months of the introductory rates, your rates can be raised to the higher rate you agreed to.

If you are more than 60 days late your rates can go up.

Interest Rate Increases apply to New Charges Only.

If your creditor increases your interest rates, the

new rate only applies to purchases following the increase. Previous balances are still at the old interest rates.

Outrageously, this makes no sense, but Credit card companies who have increased rates since Jan.1, 2009 must reconsider their reasons for those increases. If the reasons for the increases have changed they are to reduce the rate "if appropriate".

.Double Cycle Billing

Only balances in the current billing cycle can have interest charged on them.

Payments must be applied to the highest interest balances first.

Unless you have a deferred interest purchase. Such as "No interest if paid by some specific future date." They must apply your entire payment to the deferred interest program balance first.

Due Dates and Times

Your creditor must mail your bill at least 21 days prior to your due date.

Your due date must be the same every month.

The cut off time on your due date cannot be earlier than 5pm.

If your due date is on a holiday or weekend you have until 5pm of the next business day to make your payment. Exception: If your creditor has a method to process payments on holidays or weekends your payment is still due by 5pm on your due date. (Do they have a duty to tell you this? I don't see it anywhere).

High Fee Cards

If your card has fees you are required to pay like annual fees or application fees, the total of those fees cannot exceed 25% of the initial credit limit. Exception: This limit does not include penalty fees, late fees etc.

Over Limit Transactions,
You Must Opt-In or Your Card Transaction May Be Declined!!

Your creditor cannot process a transaction if it will put you over your credit limit without your permission in advance.

If your creditor allows a transaction that goes over your credit limit and you haven't opted-in for over limit transactions they can't charge you an over-limit fee.

If you opt-in for over limit transactions, your creditor can only charge you one over limit fee per billing cycle.

HOW LONG AFTER BANKRUPTCY DOES YOUR CREDIT IMPROVE?

I've never tried to get credit for anything since I filed bankruptcy, I reaffirmed on my mortgage, and never missed a mortgage payment, and I didn't file bankruptcy on a couple of department store cards that had zero balances.

I have considered refinancing my mortgage, but it has a very low adjustable rate on it now, and it can only increase or decrease by one (1%) percent per year, so I am reluctant to mess with that. It's nearly paid off at this point anyway.

Out of curiosity the other day, I ran my credit checks, and one of the credit reporting agencies was offering a free check of your credit score. I took them up on it, and found my score was 707. That's seven years after having filed bankruptcy. I'm sure this score is partly as a result of the fact I never missed a payment on my mortgage, and I didn't close out those department store credit cards. I also haven't used those department store cards in a number of years. Out of curiosity I checked, and they are still valid.

However, it's probably best if you can, not ever to use credit cards again. Instead start a savings account and put money into that.

The best thing you can do is start a savings account and exercise patience in acquiring the things you want and need. Then when you've built up a nest egg that will carry you through future times of scarcity, you can pay cash for the things you want and need.

One of the other things I've done is to buy silver and gold. Put it into a safe deposit box at the bank, but then I tend to worry about the value of the silver and gold going up and/or down! Don't worry, it does no good.

A friend suggested that if one were to prepare for a complete meltdown of the financial situation in this country, it probably wouldn't hurt to have smaller metal coins in your home to trade for goods and services if everything falls apart. All I'd have to do is clean out some purses and drawers!

WHAT CAN I DO TO AVOID GETTING IN FINANCIAL TROUBLE AGAIN

A lot of people got into trouble with credit cards, and even more got into trouble with mortgages that were extraordinarily high. As I was doing bankruptcy filings for people, I kept noticing the amounts people had in mortgages. People were getting mortgages for far more than their earnings would deem practical. They just didn't make enough money to pay them off!

My father always told me the formula for your housing, whether a rental or a purchase, should make your monthly payment no more than your weekly take home pay. I've always adhered to that formula.

Live within your means, make do with what you've got. Every day count your blessings, look around you and make a mental or actual list of all of your assets, and be grateful for them.

<u>Unconscionable Contract</u>   by Jana Lynn Shellman

WHAT IF SOMEONE TRIES TO STEAL YOUR IDENTITY?

The first thing you should understand is just how your identity can be stolen, and what you can do to prevent it. Following is from various government publications on the subject, including descriptions and methods thieves can use to steal your identity:

Identity Theft

"Publicity regarding severe cases of identity theft in the print and electronic media and portrayal of the risk of identity theft in a number of effective television commercials have raised public awareness about identity theft. Arguably, however, few persons are aware of the complexities of the many issues involved with this crime, which is really a large set of fraudulent activities ranging in size from minor swindles to major crimes using stolen identities." (Identity Theft -- A Research Review, National Institute of Justice).

Summary

Identity theft and identity fraud are terms used to refer to types of crime in which someone wrongfully obtains and uses another individual's personal data in a way that involves fraud or deception, typically for economic gain. Unlike fingerprints, which are unique to an individual and cannot be given to someone else for their use, personal data - especially Social Security numbers, bank account or credit card numbers, telephone calling card numbers, and other valuable identifying data - can be used by someone to personally profit at the victim's expense Identify Theft and Identity Fraud Web page, U.S. Department of Justice).

Unauthorized persons take funds out of others' bank or financial accounts or take over their identities altogether, running up debts and committing crimes while using the victims' names. A victim's losses may include not only out-of-pocket financial losses, but additional costs associated with trying to restore his reputation in the community and correcting erroneous information about his financial or personal status Identify Theft and Identity Fraud Web page, U.S.

Department of Justice).

According to the U.S. Federal Trade Commission (FTC) report *ID Theft: What's It All About* (2005), identity thieves use a variety of methods to gain access to your personal information. For example:

They get information from businesses or other institutions by:
stealing records from their employer,
bribing an employee who has access to these records, or
hacking into the organization's computers.
They rummage through your trash or the trash of businesses or dumps in a practice known as dumpster diving.
They obtain credit reports by abusing their employer's authorized access to credit reports or by posing as a landlord, employer, or someone else who may have a legal right to the information.
They steal credit and debit card numbers as your card is processed by using a special information storage device in a practice known as skimming.
They steal wallets and purses containing identification and credit and bank cards.

They steal mail, including bank and credit card statements, preapproved credit offers, new checks, or tax information.

They complete a "change of address form" to divert your mail to another location.

They steal personal information from your home.

They scam information from posing as a legitimate business person or government official.

New methods of identity theft continue to appear. During 2003 and early 2004, for example, a form of identity theft called phishing gained prominence. Phishing involves creating and using e-mails and Web sites designed to look like those of well-known, legitimate businesses, financial institutions, and government agencies to deceive Internet users into disclosing their personal information (e.g., bank and financial account information, usernames, passwords). The phishers then take that information and use it for criminal purposes, such as identity theft and fraud (Special Report on "Phishing", U.S. Department of Justice, 2004).

Various Federal and numerous State and local law enforcement agencies are responsible for investigating identity theft crimes. The Identity Theft

Assumption and Deterrence Act of 1998 (Public Law 105-318) made identity theft a separate crime against the person whose identity was stolen, broadened the scope of the offense to include the misuse of information as well as documents, and provided a maximum sentence of up to 25 years. Increased penalties were later prescribed for aggravated identity theft, an offense established in the Identity Theft Penalty Enhancement Act of 2004. Also, most States have enacted laws that criminalize identity theft (Identity Theft: Greater Awareness and Use of Existing Data are Needed, U.S. General Accounting Office, 2002).

Despite these actions, multijurisdictional issues - such as when a perpetrator steals personal information in one city and uses the information to conduct fraudulent activities in another city or state - and lack of training and resources, have presented challenges to law enforcement in the investigation and prosecution of complex identity cases. Because identity theft is still a "nontraditional" crime, some police departments may be unaware of the importance of taking reports of identity theft or initiating investigations (Identity Theft: Greater Awareness and Use of Existing Data are Needed, U.S. General Accounting Office, 2002).

The passage of Federal and State identity theft legislation indicates that this type of crime has been widely recognized as a serious problem across the Nation. Now, a current focus for policymakers and criminal justice administrators is to ensure that these laws are effectively enforced (Identity Theft: Greater Awareness and Use of Existing Data are Needed, U.S. General Accounting Office, 2002).

As part of its series on problem-specific guides for police, the Center for Problem-Oriented Policing has available a guide to help law enforcement professionals determine what they can do to prevent identity theft and help victims in their jurisdictions. The guide addresses identity theft, describing the problem and reviewing factors that increase the risks of it. It then identifies a series of questions to help police analyze their local problem. Finally, it reviews responses to the problem and what is known about them from evaluative research and police practice (Identity Theft, Center for Problem-Oriented Policing, 2004).

WHAT CAN I DO TO PROTECT MY IDENTITY?

Understand what the various means of stealing your identity could be, and then take all necessary steps to avoid it happening.

If you are reading this book, it is highly unlikely anyone would want to steal your credit anyway! At least that's how I looked at it until I got my credit back under control.

Unconscionable Contract   by Jana Lynn Shellman

SECURITY FREEZE

A security freeze, also known as a credit freeze, is a consumer right provided by Indiana law. There are similar laws in other states.

Placing a security freeze on your credit reports can block an identity thief from opening a new account or obtaining credit in your name. If you activate a security freeze, an identity thief cannot take out new credit in your name, even if the thief has your Social Security number or other personal information, because creditors cannot access your credit report without your permission. Placing a freeze will not lower your credit score.   Check to see if there is such a law in your State.   This is how it works in Indiana.

How to Place a Security Freeze

In Indiana, any Indiana resident can request a security freeze. There is no fee for Indiana residents to place, temporarily lift, remove or request a new password or PIN. You must place a freeze with each of the following credit reporting agencies. To place a freeze, either use each credit agency's online process or send a letter by certified mail to:

Equifax Security Freeze
P.O. Box 105788
Atlanta, GA 30348
www.freeze.equifax.com

Experian Security Freeze
P.O. Box 9554
Allen, TX 75013
www.experian.com/freeze.center.html

Trans Union Security Freeze
P.O. Box 6790
Fullerton, CA 92834-6790
www.annualcreditreporttransunion.com/fa/securityFreeze/landing

To place the freeze with each credit bureau, you may be asked to:

Provide your full name (including middle initial as well as Jr., Sr., II, III, etc.,) address, Social Security number, and date of birth;

If you have moved in the past five years, supply the addresses where you have lived over the prior five years;

Provide proof of current address such as a current utility bill or phone bill, (alternative options include a bank, insurance, or credit card statement listing your full name and address);

Provide a photocopy of a government issued identification card (state driver'd license or ID card, military identification, etc.)

If you are placing a freeze by certified mail, you may use the sample letters available online at www.IndianaConsumer.com/IDTheft

FREQUENTLY ASKED QUESTIONS

How long does it take for a security freeze to be in effect?

By Indiana law, credit reporting agencies must place a freeze within five business days from receiving your freeze request. Within ten business days of receiving your freeze request, the agencies will send you a confirmation letter containing a unique PIN (personal identification number) or password. Keep the PIN or password secured.

Can I open new credit accounts if my files are frozen?

If you want to take out a loan, get a new credit card or apply for a job or certain services, you can lift the security freeze for a certain period of time or for a specific party by notifying the credit bureau according to its procedures.

How can I remove a security freeze?

Indiana residents can have a security freeze lifted

for a specific party, temporarily or permanently, free of charge. To do so, contact the credit reporting agencies by mail, telephone or online. You must provide proper ID and your unique PIN or password. If lifting temporarily, you must include the party and/or the period of time you want your credit report to be made accessible.

How long does it take for a security freeze to be lifted?

If the requests are made by telephone or e-mail during normal business hours and under reasonable circumstances, the reporting agencies must lift the freeze within 15 minutes. If the request is made by mail, it will take three business days.

Can a creditor get my credit score if my file is frozen?

No. A creditor who requests your file from one of the three credit bureaus will only get a message or a code indicating the file is frozen.

Can I order my own credit report if my file is frozen?

Yes. You may order a free annual credit report online at www.Annual.credit.report.com

Can anyone see my credit file if it is frozen?

Your report can still be released to your existing creditors or to collection agencies acting on their own behalf. They can use it to review or collect on your account. Other creditors may use your information to make offers of credit. Government agencies may also have access in response to a court or administrative order, a subpoena, or a search warrant.

*Additional FAQs are available online at www.IndianaConsumer.com/IDTheft

ACQUIRING A PROSPERITY MIND SET

After I filed for bankruptcy, and with little or no income coming in, I went through a period where I had much fear of how I was going to make ends meet. Ends? There were no ends, there was nothing really! I didn't know how much money I could earn working from home, and had no idea if I was going to be able to go back to working in a law office.

Then I read something that gave me an idea. It said I had to get the idea of "I can't afford that." out of my head.

Shortly thereafter, I did the taxes for an old employer, and he paid me. I had a $100 bill. I put it away in my billfold where I couldn't really see it all the time. That simple act, changed my mind set. I stopped thinking "I can't afford that." Instead I began thinking, "I have that $100 in my billfold, I could buy that if I wanted it." My actual prosperity began to match my prosperity mind set. I never did spend that $100 bill, its still in my billfold, along with maybe a couple other hundreds I've stowed away in there. But I have pretty much purchased anything I wanted or needed, just because I got rid of the idea "I can't afford that."

If you're interested in my theories on positive thinking, you might want to check out my book *Winning at Wishing,* by Jana L. Shellman, which is available for Kindle at Amazon, or the paperback copy of *Winning at Wishing* which is available at Amazon, and other bookstore outlets.

You could also check out my book *The Wish Factory: How to Make Wishes Come True,* also available on Amazon Kindle, and available in trade paperback at most outlets. You might have to order it. If you cannot locate it at a bookstore, you can order it by going to www.thewishfactory.com and using PayPal.

MAKING DO WITH WHAT YOU'VE GOT

As Americans most of us are pretty lucky. Even if we've had hard times, we still have a lot to be thankful for. Look around you, and count your blessings. Learn to make do with what you've got. If something is broken, try to fix it. There are many people trying to make a living now by fixing things that are broken. Find someone who can fix things for you. It's the way our parents and grandparents survived the Great Depression.

Look around you, make a list of all of your assets. Clean out drawers, clean out the attic. Go through things that you have that you can recondition or refurbish and fix them if you can.

Just making a list of all of the things you have is a good way to count your blessings. Acknowledging your bounty is a good way to make yourself feel less poor.

There are numerous places where you can get rid of the things you don't want. Sell old books on Amazon, (I sold a "useless" book I was using for a doorstop because of its size for $200.00). There's Craigslist, and

123

other places where you can sell used items.

If you don't want to sell them, but give them away there are numerous Freecycle and Freesharing groups around the country where you can list the things you want to get rid of, and list the things you need. I once got rid of eleven giant black garbage bags full of old clothes that no longer fit. I freed up three closets!

Here are a few links to them: www.freecycle.org and www.freesharing.org

BUYING AMERICAN

We can all do our share to bring jobs back to America by buying American made products. There is a site where you can check these things out. If you are as annoyed as I am about all of the foul-smelling, toxic-smelling products that we find shipped here from China and other places, you have been reading labels the same as me.

Check out www.buyamericanmart.com   And www.buyamerican.com .

Unconscionable Contract   by Jana Lynn Shellman

REFURBISH OLD QUALITY MADE AMERICAN PRODUCTS

Until we have restored American jobs to our country, rather than buying things that appear from all over the world, I've found it's better to buy old well-made American products, and refurbish them.

For instance, I bought a printer and let my old American made printer go. I gave it away. (I wish I had kept it!) The new printer was junk. It was exactly the same brand, but it was made in China or another country. It fell apart immediately. It wouldn't do the monstrous job of printing I was used to my old printer doing. My answer to that problem was to go online and purchase a refurbished printer made in America in the 90's. I have it sitting on my desk now. It's a horse, and it does tons of work. It isn't hard to figure out. When something needs replacing, I can usually look it up on line and buy the part myself and install the part by myself. I'm not a mechanic. Thanks to the Internet, there are now YouTube videos that show you how to fix a lot of things!

Unconscionable Contract by Jana Lynn Shellman

INVENT A NEW JOB FOR YOURSELF

If you don't have a job now, you should invent a job for yourself. You've got time on your hands? Use that time to think about your life.

What hobby or pass time do you have a good time at? Is there something you could do with the knowledge you've acquired with that hobby or pass time that could be turned into a money-making proposition? Is it something you could start on a shoestring? Remember many huge corporations were begun by a dreamer who had little more than a shoestring to start with. Keep the American Dream alive, and make your own dreams come true.

Speaking of dreams, perhaps its not a hobby that could make you a new job, but perhaps it is the fulfillment of a dream come true. What have you always dreamed of doing? Is there a way to turn that into income for yourself and your family? Remember absolutely nothing is impossible, and if you can dream it, there's a way to dream it into existence.

Unconscionable Contract   by Jana Lynn Shellman

DO WHAT BRINGS YOU JOY

What things in your life bring you joy? Do you have a hobby that brings you joy?   Is there a way you can turn that joy into a job?

If you can't remember an old dream that could turn into a job, how about remembering the times you were happiest and experiencing the most joy.

Is there something about those times that you could turn into a job.

Remember the best job is one that doesn't feel like a job. The best job is one that brings you joy while you're doing it, something that you wouldn't even call "working".

Unconscionable Contract   by Jana Lynn Shellman

NON- ATTORNEY REPRESENTATION
DISCLAIMER

This book is the revelation of the author, who is not an attorney, but who took the steps outlined herein to represent herself, *in propria persona,* based upon more than fifty years of experience in a law office, as well as studies at a law school that did not lead to a degree because of intervening circumstances. None of the legal pleadings information contained herein should be considered legal advice of any sort, but should merely be viewed as the narrative and experience of an individual who applied extraordinary solutions to a common problem.

Due to the actions of the author and subsequent legal steps taken by credit card companies, and state and federal legislation, some of these solutions are no longer valid, and some of the resulting legislation has altered the way credit card companies do business.

The contents of this book should be viewed as interesting information only, and not as legal advice. If you believe some of the solutions might work for you, you should seek the advice of an attorney in that regard.

Furthermore, nothing contained in this book should be construed as legal advice, or steps that could be taken by you.

Provided, however, that the information with regard to the Credit Reporting Agencies, and the Fair Debt Collection Practices in dealing with Debt Collectors, is valid, and the letter to the debt collectors and bankruptcy forms are information that is available on line and not information that requires an attorney to access.

As the author instructs: **Do Not Try This At Home.** If you are having problems with debt collectors, or are in need of the advice of a bankruptcy attorney, please seek professional assistance. Again, If you believe some of the solutions might work for you, you should seek the advice of an attorney in that regard. Furthermore, nothing contained in this book should be construed as legal advice, or steps that could be taken by you. Thank you.

Unconscionable Contract   by Jana Lynn Shellman

Made in United States
Orlando, FL
22 February 2025

58798524R00083